Interviewing & Hiring Software Performance Test Professionals

James Pulley

Founded in 2012, PerfBytes mission is to help software performance professionals improve the value of delivery to stakeholders of performance: end users of applications, product owners, quality assurance organizations. The views expressed in its publications are entirely those of the authors and do not necessarily reflect the views of the staff, owners, or pets of PerfBytes
`https://www.perfbytes.com` `http://press.perfbytes.com`

PerfBytes Press, An Imprint of Journeyman Publishing LLC
111 Foster Mill Circle. Pauline, South Carolina 29374 USA

Editor: Rachel Laney `rachel@press.perfbytes.com`
          Joanna Im Titus Chevraux `joanna@press.perfbytes.com`
Errata: `Errors@press.perfbytes.com`

First Edition, 2021. Cataloging-in-Publication Data is available from the Library of Congress.

Paperback: ISBN 978-0-9885402-6-2
eBook: ISBN 978-0-9885402-7-9
Hardback: ISBN 978-0-9885402-8-6

Journeyman Publishing is a speciality publisher for Cybersecurity, IT Professional Services, Software Performance Engineering, Technical Selling, & Software Quality Assurance books. If you have an interest in becoming a published writer, please contact us at:

111 Foster Mill Circle, Pauline South Carolina 29374 USA
newauthor@journeymanpublishing.com

To my lovely bride, Rachel.

Without your support this work would not be possible.

jpulley@localhost ≫ whoami

I have had a career filled with good fortune. Before I graduated from **Furman University**[1] I had already been exposed to enterprise class software and the challenges associated with running software performance across integrated networks. I found myself at **Microsoft** upon graduation, with tours through OS, desktop database, and server database support organizations where my architecture, troubleshooting, and communications skills were honed.

Since that time I have worked for a number of vendors: **Banyan Systems** (Global network solutions and directory services), **Gigalabs** (providers of super computer network infrastructures), **Mercury Interactive** (now **Micro Focus**), **Ganymede Software** software (now Ixia). Both Ganymede and Mercury focused on different aspects of performance testing, network and application respectively.

From 2001–2017 I operated either as an independent consultant or a member of a Value Added Reseller (VAR) management team, focused on helping customers solve difficult performance issues. Clients have ranged from medium–sized businesses to some of the largest financial institutions, governments, and service providers in the world. Since 2002, if you have booked a flight, obtained a mortgage, crossed an international border, or shopped online, then our paths have crossed in the I.T. ether.

After the events of Sept 11, 2001, I had some downtime. I began to give back online, addressing questions regarding testing, process, tools, and techniques in public forums. Along the way I have been asked to moderate a number of areas on **Yahoo Groups**, **SQAForums**, LinkedIn, **Google Groups**, & Facebook related to tools, performance testing, or performance

---

[1]https://www.furman.edu/. Computer Science–Business. 1991.

processes. I have answered over 10,000 questions online during this time. This book is a continuation of that act of giving back to the community.

In 2012, Mark Tomlinson and I founded **PerfBytes**, a podcast focused on improving the technical skills and value of delivery of performance testing services in the market. PerfBytes tackles topics as diverse as patterns, technologies, tools, and training — all with a goal towards improving delivery in performance engineering services.

Late 2017, I joined the professional services organization of **TEKsystems Global Services** as a Practice Manager for their new Performance Engineering group. I currently lead a group of amazing individuals who accomplish performance engineering miracles on an ongoing basis. As their manager, it is my privilege to help them remove barriers to their success. They drive me to be a better manager. In turn, I ask each of them to become better engineers and architects.

Through this work I have met incredible people whose paths I would never have crossed otherwise. For some I have had the rare privilege of being the first to recognize their talents, to help cultivate their skills and introduce them to this very odd profession, one where we find the things that others miss. A man can never be poor who is surrounded by friends — I will never be a poor man.

Thank you for purchasing this book, allowing me to work in a profession I love, where my odd mix of skills and talents allows me to provide positive impacts in the lives of so many. One that has provided opportunities I would not have imagined for myself when I graduated from college.

Forward

"Anyone can be an effective performance tester with tool 'X'!"

April 1, 1996, I joined Mercury Interactive. Mercury was growing like crazy at the time. As the engineering part of the sales team, I was guilty of being where that very message was delivered to customers as part of the sales process. The message was teamed with a very seductive product demonstration I drove. That demonstration walked through the usage of functional test automation, test management, and performance testing tools in a fast hour.

The demo was sexy. It was paired with the right messages for management. Truth is, the messages were designed to remove barriers to the purchase of products. No one likes to be told that you will need to pair this tool with someone who already understands how to find performance issues; that is the unfortunate truth of the matter and why we are here today.

Cue the classical iceberg diagram in *Figure 1*. Tool skills represent ten percent or less of the skills required to be successful as a performance tester, engineer, or architect. There is no mistaking that tool skills are critical skills. Without them, an accurate and effective test cannot be constructed. Underpinning tool skills, there is a large set of foundational skills which are essential in order to be able to use the available tools on the market effectively to generate load and to find performance issues. Being able to diagnose the **root cause** of poor performance is the path to deliver value in the process, and ultimately to have applications which are considerably more responsive and scalable than before.

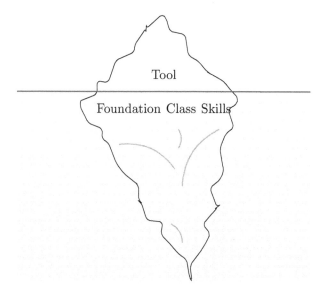

Figure 1: *Foundations Iceberg Chart*

This lack of understanding of the core **foundation skills** involved in the performance engineering discipline is where the vast majority of people who are not already in the performance field struggle in identification and vetting of candidates. Recruiters and interviewers concentrate their efforts on tools listed on a résumé, rather than on the foundational skills which are the greater indicator of success in the field. When it becomes difficult to find a candidate who can deliver value, organizations often resort to socially promoting a person from another area of software quality assurance without understanding the foundations of success.

Since 1996 I have been interviewing, hiring, and mentoring individuals to be successful in the delivery of performance services to customers. It is difficult to find individuals with the right mix of skills to be successful. Hopefully, this book will provide some insight into the types of individuals and the skills required to be successful in this discipline, across both commercial and **open–source** tools.

Should you accept the insights from this book, the information will save you from *at least one* bad hire for a performance role. On that basis alone, this book is a bargain! Chapter 1 will provide some insight into just how expensive a poor hire in performance can become.

There are a few conventions associated with this book. Where you see a term or phrase **bolded** within a sentence, check the Glossary. For anything that might be considered jargon, I have tried to cobble together a definition to clarify. You may also find items *emphasized* for your attention. <u>Underlined references</u> refer to other sections within this book. All of the links to external references are also managed by PerfBytes Press rather than going direct. And, because of the influence of Monty Python on PerfBytes, you might see an occasional giant cartoon hand reference. These are items for monumentally massive special attention in Python parlance.

- Managing the redirect for the destination allows us to update a link in case the relevant information ever moves without having to print another book.

- If we find a better link on a topic, such as for the discussion of "percentile," then we can update that link transparently, providing additional value for your investment in this book.

- Vendors do consolidate or merge. By managing the links on the back-end, we can redirect an existing reference to the most current information.

- Many vendors are referenced in this book. It is possible that a vendor or an organization listed may want a specific landing page for readers of this book related to the delivery of value with their tools. We have the ability to redirect to an appropriate landing page without requiring you to repurchase the book for updated links.

By managing external links for current data, we are able to provide you with a document that will stay up-to-date and will provide beneficial information for a long time.

If you do find that there is a better link than one we have used for a topic, or a link which has gone stale/dead, please drop us an email note to `mailto:linkupdates@press.perfbytes.com` with the name of the book, page number, and reference for update

Why the large margins? I have a habit as I read books of highlighting & making my own annotations in the margins. I have included a generous outside margin to support others who engage in the same behavior. Go Crazy! It's your book now.

Contents

List of Figures

1

Who Is This Book For?

- Recruiters

- Interviewers

- Personnel Managers

- Organizational Contacts For Outsourced Skills

- Product Owners

This book is for you. To enable you to accurately identify the skills you need and to interview for those skills successfully.

The site *Polydelic*[1] in a 2020 blog post suggests the cost of hiring a bad developer tops 400,000 USD. When you take into account the secondary costs associated with that bad hire —the cleanup organizationally, additional project costs due to delay/rework, the cost of defects which escape to production, . . . —is it accurate? I leave that for you to judge. I am including the reference here as a marker of sorts to show the impact of one bad hire, a developer.

---

[1] press.perfbytes.com/books/jp/interview/Polydelic

What is the cost of a poor performance hire? I would argue it is substantially more than the developer. Performance defects that are not caught, and allowed to slip through to production, have all sorts of costly effects:

- Lost productivity due to slow systems.

- Increase in help desk calls related to "system is slow" and associated follow up.

- Increase in *server outage* events related to high load conditions. What is an hour of down time worth to your organization?

- Lost sales and lost customers in eCommerce environments.

In March of 2020, governments around the world found that their unemployment insurance systems began to fail under the unprecedented load associated with layoffs related to the SARS–COV–19 (COVID) pandemic. Elected officials ordered businesses to close for a period of time in an effort to halt the spread of the disease. At the same time, elected officials waved any waiting period associated with applying for government support in response to layoffs.

This led to a *run on the bank*. Users who would normally arrive in small numbers, randomly as a result of natural layoff patterns, instead arrived all at once. This is a condition for which systems are rarely designed. In performance engineering, we refer to this condition as a 'point,' or 'spot,' load. Sites failed. Sites continued to fail as waves of users came back as soon as the sites returned to service. In some cases, it took months before the cresting waves of user load subsided to a point where systems were considered to no longer be under stress.

The State of Florida (USA) was particularly hard hit by these system failures. After an investigation, a preliminary report by the State's Inspector General found that the site had not been effectively tested, with tests rising to only 4200 users of the target 200,000 user load[2]. In the case of the State of Florida, the costs of poor performance led to an immediate expenditure of over 100 Million USD to handle the load[3] of increased applications for benefits. This is followed by an expected additional expenditure of between 70 and 240 Million USD in the years 2021–2025 to 'fix' the existing system.[4] The initial system cost was less than 90 million USD.

---

[2]press.perfbytes.com/books/jp/interview/FLIG
[3]press.perfbytes.com/books/jp/interview/clickorlando
[4]press.perfbytes.com/books/jp/interview/orlandosentinel

Florida's challenge in performance testing illustrates our industry problem well. Either these were brand new performance testers who struggled to deliver value, or they were experienced performance testers who failed to deliver value. Those who were managing the performance testing effort did not have enough specific working knowledge on performance testing or performance engineering practices to recognize the risk associated with the poor work product.

I know you were not expecting a horror novel when you picked up this book. This is as close as it gets. Poor work product. Unrecognized Risks. Millions of dollars in emergency costs, even exceeding the cost of the original system. Governments have a financial stopgap when systems fail to perform, the taxpayers. For a commercial enterprise, poor performance of a multi-million dollar critical system in production often becomes a fatal corporate event. Odds are, these same performance testers have been used to test other systems. Do you believe the value delivered to those customers was any greater than the value delivered to the State of Florida? Are you sufficiently terrified of that answer?

Back to my earlier statement: One poor performance tester is many times more expensive than a poor developer. Case in point: State of Florida!

Performance Architects, **Performance Engineers**, and **Performance Testers** do not generally work on just one application or system: Their skills are rare within a company. Project the costs of that one poor hire across multiple applications or systems within an enterprise. The direct and indirect project costs, and opportunity costs associated with poor performance efforts scale quickly.

Software performance is a profession where patterns of application use, system resource use, and configuration play large roles in determining performance. Without a collection of "lore" built up from solving problems, or a model with which to evaluate new ones, a performance professional may be at a loss to find, or explain the nature of the problem, or to recommend a fix.

A lack of understanding on how to diagnose a performance issue impacts the majority of performance personnel on the market today. We'll get to why that is the case a little later.

You may be thinking, "Holy cow! Did he just say the majority of the people engaging in performance activities today can't find root cause?"

Yes. I did.

I have twenty years of data to back up this statement. From my experience as a moderator for up to a dozen forums on quality assurance tools, processes, and practices, it has been my observation that the vast majority of people being brought to the performance profession are not provided opportunities for training. They are not provided mentors for continued professional development. *No one is vetting them for their foundation skills.*

These individuals have fundamental skill challenges which hinder their ability to deliver tangible value in performance engagements. A substantial number of these individuals lack basic research skills involving the use of online product manuals (even the ability to find identical questions asked) which are searchable by Google and other search engines. Would you ever hire a **Java** developer that doesn't know Java to deliver a product on an accelerated schedule? This happens all too often for users of performance testing tools, promoted into the role.

As a product owner, a QA manager, or an engineering lead, if you have ever received a report on **response times** (taken directly from a test tool) as the report for a performance testing engagement, without explanation or analysis — not even a note on whether the test was repeatable — you understand this scale of the industry–wide problem. If you have ever looked at the report and asked, "What does this mean?" then this problem of value in delivery is obvious to you.

For recruiters, you need methods to identify these individuals to avoid a poor hiring decision. So too do individuals charged with interviewing candidates. As a highly specialized field, interviewers often do not have specific working knowledge on performance testing or performance engineering practices to be able to vet candidates effectively. Engineering managers in charge of personnel and ensuring quality in the delivery of performance services also need a better understanding of quality candidates. Candidates often rely on having just slightly more performance testing domain knowledge than those interviewing them. Software performance is an exotic practice, so this deception becomes easy to pull off.

Hang on tight! This is going to be a fast and wild ride through the market for performance test personnel designed to get you up to speed quickly in effective interviewing and hiring the right people for the job.

2

Who Do You need?

Most people, when they think of a software performance professional, immediately think of a performance tester. This is usually someone who is a member of the quality assurance group within a company. These individuals usually have a software testing need. This need is either to test a pre-production application, or to test an application which has failed to perform in production. An application needs a test!

It is worthwhile to stop and consider what is the desired outcome of that effort. The answer will often determine the type of individual you need to solicit on the open market. Is the goal a simple reproduction of load? Is the goal to be able to diagnose issues within the application? What about identifying larger patterns in the design and deployment? All of these may be desired, but they require different classes of performance professionals.

- A Performance Tester is someone who is capable of producing a test from a set of requirements. This individual doesn't necessarily have the skills to collect and vet requirements, nor analyze test data for root cause. They are well–versed in tool mechanical skills.

The recruiting market concentrates on tool skills.

- A Performance Engineer builds on the tool skills of the Performance Tester. They are able to work with the customer to define requirements, design tests to meet those requirements, and analyze the results of tests for issues. Often a performance engineer can make recommendations to improve performance without ever running a test based upon observations collected from functional tests or production. Performance engineers are data–driven. You can also find them not attached to quality assurance organizations at all, but as part of operations personnel, or even as "that long-bearded guy with the goofy pocket protectors" — The one that the company keeps around to solve problems.

- A Performance Architect is a super–set of the previous two categories. This individual is able to identify areas of risk at the design and business requirements stages, with the ability to make recommendations which reduce risk and improve performance of the application.

You will need at least a Performance Engineer to obtain *value* from your performance testing efforts. The analytical skills associated with the performance architect and engineering roles are critical to understanding why an application is not performing as expected. *Value* is delivered as part of the test findings during the analysis of performance test results.

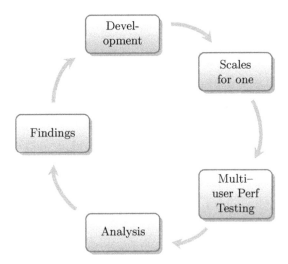

Figure 2.1: *Performance Process Flow*

It is in the analysis phase where actual value can be obtained in performance efforts. A **performance test** *is simply a* *mechanism for the production of data.* A multi–user performance test exists to generate measurements of response time within the system, and measurements of resource use at defined intervals. A challenge on access to resources is the cause when a response time is slow. We will examine this in more detail later, in the next chapter, The Performance Test.

Your Funnel

What does the market for performance professionals look like? Here I will be airing some more profession bad news:

- Half of all résumés for performance testers and engineers are fraudulent. This extends to fake profiles on LinkedIn and paid referral services using VoIP redirects.

  You're probably thinking, "James, that's a bold statement. How could you possibly know that?" For the better part of two decades I worked in the Value Added Reseller (VAR) Community defining solutions for delivery to customers. As part of those efforts, we often were required to build teams of individuals with performance skills to address the customers' needs. For one customer alone we vetted over 1000 individuals by résumé examination, a subset of those for interviews, with less than 25 being hired. We still needed seven more skilled testers. We went to the market to hire for individuals with strong foundational skills — We provided training to close the gap. Pouring through hundreds of résumés, LinkedIn profiles, and other data sources was not uncommon in order to find a handful of skilled individuals.

  Data from constant sampling of the market to find skilled individuals for services delivery underpins these ratios. While the numbers of applicants changed over time, the ratios held.

  Just how bad is it? I have received my own résumé back with someone else's name at the top. I know others who have received their own résumés back as well. When you find these individuals and organizations representing them, please consider the blackball policies in your organization to protect you from future efforts orchestrated by the same organizations or individuals.

50%

- Of the remainder, forty percent of all résumés are from individuals who have not benefited from training or a mentor. This includes tool training.

How does this happen? This is the result of social promotion of developers into the performance role. Most often this is because of a billing need by an outsourced QA organization. A smaller ratio comes from in-house promotions from the ranks of automated functional testers. If the individual survives the trial-by-fire, then they will be allowed to work in performance again. These individuals can go years without delivering value beyond some level of tool capability. What are some of the characteristics to look for here?

90%

1. A résumé which shows a bouncing back and forth between functional and performance roles. (Performance roles where value is delivered are specialized roles.)

2. A high résumé concentration on tool mechanical skills focusing on tool features rather than outcomes of performance efforts.

3. A profound weakness in application architecture, from communications protocols to monitoring of systems.

4. References can speak to their tool capability, perhaps even team fit, but are unable to speak to a direct performance problem that the candidate identified or solved.

- This leaves about ten percent of the population who possess the foundational skills for the job, have been trained, mentored, and have a demonstrable track record for high value delivery. Of which, about 2.5 percent are available for hire or are looking to move.

$97\frac{1}{2}\%$

Make no mistake, these individuals understand their rarity in the market. They are the ones charged with cleaning up after the failures of the fraudsters and fractionally-skilled inside of organizations. It is often the recruiter who does not understand the rarity because of a concentration on tool mechanics vs foundational skills.

Expect a conversion rate on the funnel of about 30:1. For every thirty candidates, you will find one with the value required to extend an offer.

Economic Oddities

All of this fraud and low–value delivery has led to an odd economic condition: Even as the demand for performance engineering personnel has risen over the past two decades, the compensation rates for open positions have declined. This is true even where positions for performance professionals stay open for months on end. I know of one company that had an opening which went unfilled for well over a year. In a time of sparse labor availability, it is the natural condition for labor rates to rise to reflect the scarcity of the skills. Why is that not the case for this market?

I have had the opportunity to speak with several economists about this condition. Their responses are identical: This condition of declining rates at the same time of skills scarcity only occurs when the value of the skills available is so low that it overcomes the natural tendency of rates to rise. As Walt Kelly's character Pluperfect Pogo once noted, "We Have Met the Enemy and He Is Us."[1]

With so much fraud and low–value delivery, there are organizations which have never encountered a high–value performance architect, performance engineer, or performance tester. These organizations have simply adjusted their rates of payment to reflect the actual value received, typically over multiple generations of personnel in a similar delivery role. Where you have a client who views performance personnel as commoditized resources, with low to middling return, now you understand the basis for their observations.

Systems Reliability Engineer (SRE)

With the rise of DevOps, a new role has arrived on the scene which shares some attributes with traditional performance personnel, particularly Performance Architects: the System Reliability Engineer, or **SRE**. As the term Software Development Engineer in Test (SDET) arrived on the scene via Microsoft, the SRE arrives courtesy of Google.

Following the Google definition, an SRE should spend half of their time in development and the other half in operations. If that bias shifts on a consistent basis, the individual should become pinned to the area where shift has occurred. As an example, if the consistent bias is to development, the individual should shift to full–time development. Likewise, for operations. In practice it is very difficult to maintain this 50:50 balance between the two sides of the house.

---

[1]`press.perfbytes.com/books/jp/interview/pogo`

Skill	Architect	Engineer	SRE	Tester
Development	A	A	✓	
SaaS/PaaS Contract Review	A			
Architecture Review	✓			
Monitoring Strategy	✓	✓	✓	
Perf Requirements	✓	✓		
Perf Test Plan	✓	✓		
Perf Test Development	✓	✓		✓
Perf Test Execution	✓	✓	✓	✓
Perf Test Analysis	✓	✓	V	
Log Analysis	✓	✓	✓	
Load Profile Development	✓	✓		
Perf Improvements	✓	✓	V	
Ops Improvements	✓	V	✓	
Capacity Planning	✓			
Mathematical Modeling	✓			
Simulations/Interface Stubs	V	V	✓	
Lead Performance Efforts	✓	✓		
Integrate with DevOps Pipeline	✓	✓	✓	
Project Budgeting/Forecasting	✓	✓		
Cross Group Communication	✓	V	V	

Figure 2.2: *Role Capabilities Table*

A Advisory Role   V Varies by Candidate

You may be thinking, "OK, James. This is all well and good. But what is the point of bringing up this SRE role?"

SRE's are being asked to take on the same diagnostic roles for performance issues as traditional performance engineers and architects, as well as fixing the issues. SRE's suffer from the same career development model as effective performance personnel: lack of cultivation of foundational skills, training on tools and processes, and mentoring for a period of time. Tasked with being fifty-percent developer, these individuals also face issues associated with inadequate education for developers on what drives poor application performance. Universities will speak generously on the topics of Moore's Law or the use of on–demand scaling within the cloud, but very little attention is paid to how resource use drives poor response time and scalability.

The smaller your performance engineering & testing team, the higher the skill level required from each individual team member. As a performance team expands beyond a half a dozen individuals, it becomes easier to bring in junior individuals to grow in the role, knowing they will begin with tool mechanics as a performance tester, then move into a performance engineer role as they acquire more soft and hard skills. From there, a migration to SRE or performance architect is viable.

The usual retention period for a new entrant to the profession is 18-24 months. The skill uplift makes them considerably more valuable to the market. If you seek to retain a person as they near the eighteen-month mark, you should consider making a market adjustment to their compensation as a proactive measure.

When you write your next set of performance role requirements, consider concentrating more on outcomes and capabilities versus particular tool skills. Figure 2.2 notes the capabilities you should expect from each type of resource.

There are patterns in organizations which should dictate one type of candidate over another, such as selecting an Engineer over a straight Tester, or an Architect over an Engineer. The flowchart below attempts to capture major patterns which should compel an organization to select one type of position over another for purposes of delivery in performance testing efforts. The Questions Legend is as follows:

Resource Flowchart Legend

These questions apply to the flowchart on the facing page.

1. Is this a team of one Performance Tester?

2. Are the performance requirements present at the start of the project? Are these requirements used by all members of the development, architecture, and platform engineering teams for application design & construction?

3. Is the time for performance efforts sized using the requirements? Or, is a fixed project time allotted, such as two weeks?

4. Does your organization need analysis of the results, including potential root cause for performance issues?

5. Do you need an individual capable of leading performance engagements?

6. Do you just need someone on a team to build and run tests? A tool mechanic?

7. The smaller the team, the more capable each person has to be. Specialization into dedicated tool users begins at around six team members.

The questions are numbered in *Figure 2.3 Architect, Engineer, or Tester Decision Tree* on the facing page from 1 to 7 above.

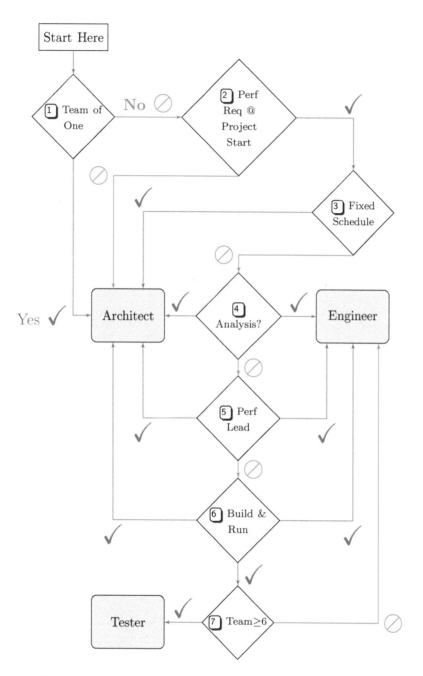

Figure 2.3: *Architect, Engineer, or Tester Decision Tree*

3

The Performance Test

What is a Performance Test? A **performance test** is part of a very broad category of tests that are concerned with response time, the use of resources, or both.

The response time for a system is an indication of how resources are used. When a resource is allocated, when it is collected, how large the resource allocation is, or even how often the resource is accessed, all drive the end result: response time. When a huge file passes across the network, response time increases. On Black Friday 2019. one eCommerce provider included a 45 megabyte image file on the front page of their website, resulting in a dramatically increased response time. To be fair, it was a beautiful image. Unfortunately, not enough people had an opportunity to see it — the site went down. Do you have a complex, embedded sub–query which is hit 10,000 times to produce a result? The results will slow.

Please bear with me while I delve into technical details. There is a method behind the madness. Figure 3.1, *Standard Performance Engineering Model*, sets a framework for discussions on how resources are being used.

CPU, Disk, RAM, and Network: We refer to these elements as the **finite resource pool**. These are the physical limits of a host that all software needs to operate within. You may have heard of the phrase, **autoscaling**, in reference to the cloud. This is the

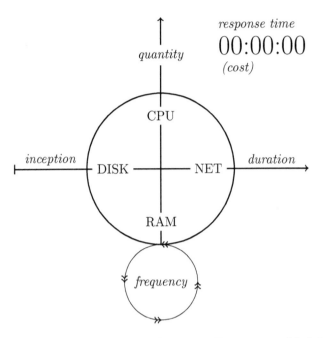

Figure 3.1: *Standard Performance Engineering Model*

ability of a virtual machine, a virtualized PC running in a cloud data center, to increase the limits of CPU, RAM, or both, when thresholds are hit for usage. Likewise, you may have heard of the term, **resource leak**. This is when an application allocates a resource, but fails to deallocate the resource to make it available to the rest of the system for use. This most commonly occurs with memory, leading to a need to reboot servers (or virtual machines, Java VM, .NET VM, ...) on a regular basis.

 There is an axiom in performance engineering: *Bad code scales to fill the available resource pool.*

Even with autoscaling enabled to increase your pool size, inefficient code will cause the need to scale again and again, until you hit the limit of available machine size. This reliance upon the use of autoscaling to address performance issues is many times more expensive in production than finding a skilled performance professional who can identify the issues before production. Autoscaling is a premium-priced feature for cloud providers with the intention of being an emergency measure for exceptional events, not a standard item which is accessed frequently.

Coming back to the definition of a performance test, the questions reference response time and resources. We can ask these questions at any point in the life cycle of an application, across any scale. We can ask a question on response time and resources for something as small as a single execution of a unit test: "Is it within specification for response time?" If it is not, then the question becomes, "Why not?"

Invariably the cause boils down to how much resource time is being taken by the code. It could be something simple such as extended logging for debug purposes, hitting the disk too often, or something more complex. Perhaps what is needed is a change to a function call for the calculation of a percentile to be slightly less precise, but within the needs of the business requirements. These examples come directly from observations of clients.

There is a second axiom: *That which will not scale for one user shall not scale for many.* In essence, if your response times are not acceptable for a single user running alone on the system, they will not be any better when you add multiple users.

A **Business Process**, a page, a microservice, or a unit test component which does not meet response time requirements for a single–user execution will not meet the same requirements as multiple users begin execution of the same code. The timed event may begin to slow with the addition of as few as one more user. Each additional user added increases the odds that a competition or contention of a common resource will occur. Performance cannot be "tested in." Performance must be a part of the application design.

As with many other areas of information technology, the **Pareto Principle** has applications in software performance engineering. Project managers look to those small numbers of critical path items which cause eighty percent of the delays. Developers spend eighty percent of their time on the twenty percent of the code which is highly complex. Eighty percent of performance issues can be resolved just by ensuring that items to be tested meet all performance requirements for single-user execution. Far too often, a performance question is never asked regarding response time or resource usage until two users are run together as part of multiuser performance testing. At that point there is a large amount of technical debt to unwind to get to a performant state.

Where to start? Does your organization have a standard set of performance requirements that are in place at the inception of projects? If not, then I would refer you to the standards offered by Google as part of the Google **RAIL** model.[1]

Let's now build upon the information above. For most organizations, the types of performance tests they wish to conduct involve the reproduction of the load from production. Either this load is a prediction of what is expected to be in place for a new application, or this load is derived from observations in production.

Whether the test is of a single user or of 200,000 users all hitting a website at the same time to purchase a copy of a dress a member of the royal family was just seen wearing, the same questions apply:

- How long did the system take to respond for each of the critical events (login, item page, checkout, ...)?

- Then, for each of the finite resources:

    1. When was the resource allocated?
    2. How large was the allocation?
    3. How often was the resource accessed?
    4. When was the resource deallocated, or returned to the pool for other processes to use?

The testing tools that are used to build multi–user tests are dedicated, integrated development environments. Test code, often referred to as scripts, is used to represent the behavior of an end–user in navigation of an application or interface. Tools are used to manage the substitution of user entered data, the management of dynamic data returned from the application infrastructure, and to collect and organize test results. These tools require the same development skills you would expect from any other member of your development team.

---

[1]press.perfbytes.com/books/jp/interview/rail

Dude! I Just Need Someone Who Can Run A Test!

Performance Engineering, and its sub-discipline Performance Testing, are considered exotic practices. Organizations struggle to understand what to interview for in terms of tools and skills. The current model, as evidenced by the high level of fraud and low–skilled individuals, has not served our industry well.

This background information is a deliberate attempt to simplify what information performance professionals collect and the types of questions which are asked.

At the end of this book, you should be able to comfortably interview a candidate without having to study a battery of questions about a particular tool. You should be able to make decisions on the quality of the candidate you are interviewing, understanding whether or not they possess the foundational skills required to deliver on the tasks you expect and the value desired by your organization.

Where Is Value Added In The Process?

A test generates load. While under load, we collect measurements of time. Measurements of time are referred to by various tool makers as **timing records** or **transactions**. We also collect resource measurements so we can ask questions when a response time is too long, or is termed "out of spec." Without an understanding of how resources are used, it becomes impossible to ask or answer critical questions.

You have likely noticed that several times I have already referred to this notion of *value* in performance efforts. We can collect measurements of time and resources out of production. So, why go through the expense of building a performance test? We want to be able to ask those questions of, "Why?" and "How to fix it?"

This is where value is generated in the performance testing effort: Not in the production of the test, but in the analysis of what happened when the requirements were not met. Understanding the why and how to fix the issue has particular value in avoiding the consequences of poor performance or an outage in production, where the cost of a defect is substantially higher than just before they go live.[2]

---

[2]**The Economic Impacts of Inadequate Infrastructure for Software Testing**. NIST. May 2002. press.perfbytes.com/books/jp/

The mark of value in performance engineering & testing efforts is the identification of an issue which negatively impacts response time or scalability, along with enough data for development to further isolate for a fix, if not enough data to fix completely. When analysis is cut off, or does not occur, then there is no opportunity for value delivery. You are left with data generation and some statistical information.

4

Foundations

As noted at the end of the last chapter, interviewing for performance has an exotic flair to it. Not a lot of people specialize in this field. And, let's face it, colleges and universities don't usually cover the topic — unless it's in reference to **Moore's Law** or using autoscaling in the cloud. By breaking down the core foundational skills of a performance professional into common areas where your organization already has expertise, you should be able to leverage internal individuals with comparable skills to evaluate candidates.

Understanding the foundational skills which lead to success in performance efforts should level the playing field between the organization that is interviewing and the candidates interviewed. Fraudulent candidates rely upon the grounding of performance engineering & testing as exotic practices. They know this exotic nature often leaves organizations reliant upon interviewing for tool mechanical skills. Candidates study banks of tool questions, knowing that interviewers often study the same banks of questions found online, as part of interview preparation.

Abraham Maslow[1] wrote about a hierarchy of needs with self–actualization at the peak. With apologies to Mr. Maslow, I am going to illustrate a set of technical dependencies which lead to value in the delivery of performance testing at the top of the pyramid. Without strong foundation skills, a candidate will be unable to construct effective tests, independent of tool. Without effective tests, data is compromised for analysis. Lacking the ability to analyze effectively cuts off the path to deliver value. This chapter will cover multiple classes of foundation skills which are key to the success of performance personnel.

Figure 4.1 illustrates this dependency set. Value is realized when the findings are integrated back into the application as changes to architecture, code, or configuration for the improvement of performance.

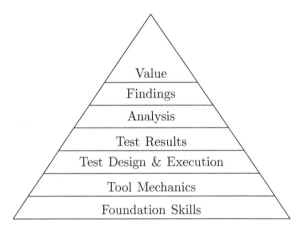

Figure 4.1: *Value Dependencies in Performance Testing*

Role Legend

At the start of each section, a key will be included to denote which particular skills are required of each role:

A	Performance Architect	T	Performance Tester
E	Performance Engineer	S	Systems Reliability Engineer (SRE)

---

[1]press.perfbytes.com/books/jp/interview/maslow

Architecture

Ⓐ Ⓔ Ⓢ

A weakness here will destroy value in delivery of performance testing services quickly. Candidates need to understand where and how to collect a measurement of resources and response times. The collection of response times item is straightforward - all performance testing tools will collect this. Collecting resource measurements is trickier. Performance personnel need to be able to articulate a strategy on where and how to collect time and resource measurements from many segments of the application architecture: Physical, Logical, and Virtual. Examples:

- CPU, Disk, RAM, & Network from shared resources at the hypervisor level for an operating system virtual machine solution such as **VMware**.

- Resource measurements for an operating system virtual machine guest running on VMware. It may be required to get some measurements from the hypervisor for accuracy.

- Measurements of free memory from inside of a Java Virtual Machine running inside of the VMware Guest operating system virtual machine..

- Measurements associated with compiles (CPU), cache hits (Disk/RAM), table scans (Disk), bytes sent/received (Network) from a database server, running inside of the Java Virtual Machine, which itself is a guest to an OS which is running as a VMware virtual machine.

  DB ↔ Java ↔ OS (Guest) ↔ VMware ↔ Hardware

Just to be clear, this is a bit of an absurd example. Performance would be poor. Every resource request would need to be brokered through multiple tiers, with an associated prioritization and cost. Multiple layers of resource arbitration does represent the resource access model you would find running a database inside of Java for a cloud provider. Such providers include Amazon AWS, Microsoft Azure, and the Google Cloud.

The architecture of the application or system under test drives how tests are implemented for the collection of response times. Until 2015, most performance testing work was delivered at the protocol level: HTTP, Oracle database, SAP, Sockets, and many others. Modern development models with thick **JavaScript** frameworks (**React**, ...) for the web have made continuing to test at the protocol level very difficult. Having an understanding of client architecture, how and where response times are measured, impacts both tool selection and the development model for the reproduction of a business process within a test tool.

Your candidate should be very comfortable discussing application architecture, how architecture drives monitoring decisions, as well as how application architecture drives tool appropriateness. Mature performance personnel are naturally curious folk. Discussions surrounding applications, monitoring, and tools, should wind up with the candidate turning tables on the interviewer, asking questions to find out more about the environment and the applications to be tested in order to determine a technical path for test construction and execution.

The ability to switch discussion from the physical constructs to the logical layers is an excellent test of abstract thought for the candidate. The ability to think abstractly comes into play not only in architecture, but in test design, as well as working through process issues in **Waterfall**, **Agile**, **Scaled Agile**, or other development models.

Monitoring extensibility

Performance testing tools are by their nature extensible. These tools are built around general purpose programming languages and include the ability to integrate with third–party tools, such as **deep diagnostic** tools for .Net and *Java* environments. This extensibility allows for test–tool generated requests to be tracked through a Java or .Net virtual machine, with the request being profiled for cost at each section of code. This is an incredibly powerful feature which allows for easy drill–down within a deep diagnostic tool to better understand where time is being spent in a particular section of code. This type of integration may be accomplished with every HTTP/WEB protocol testing tool on the market via the integration of a custom header during test development.

Some commercial tools have even deeper levels of integration. One example is Tricentis **NeoLoad**, whose **Dynatrace** integration allows for the viewing of ongoing performance test results live through the Dynatrace console. Other tools, such as **Micro Focus LoadRunner**, are able to integrate the data from deep diagnostic tools into its own result set for drill down purposes. Both models allow for easier integration of complex data for the identification of performance issues in code.

Monitoring extensibility also applies to open–source tools. The current open–source performance testing tool kits for generating load are unitaskers – They generate load and little else. The tasks of monitoring, integration of the monitored data with timing records, analysis, and reporting are left to additional tools. As an example, we will use **JMeter**. JMeter is a load driver. In order to integrate data from other sources, you need a common broker for the multiple sets of data.

That common broker becomes **Grafana**. Grafana then also pulls monitor data using **Prometheus**. That time series data is then analyzed either in Grafana or exported to another tool such as the statistical package **R** for the analysis of data. R might also be used for graphing and statistical reporting. Reports are generated from JMeter, Grafana, R, or perhaps a consolidation tool such as **Tableau**.

How does this impact your interviewing a candidate? *If you are using an open–source tool then you need to consider the full tool chain for expertise during the interview, not just the load driver.*

Communications Skills

A E

Performance architects and performance engineers are going to have to work with the business to collect and vet requirements, returning with business level analysis after tests complete. Architects and engineers will need to work with the enterprise architecture team for information on the application under test. They will need to work with operations personnel for system configuration and monitoring information. They will need to communicate project status with Project Managers or Scrum Masters using correct language. The ability to communicate in a model appropriate to multiple roles is a premium skill. Your candidate will be communicating with many audiences, with many working models, and with numerous levels of jargon across your enterprise.

Within one room, the person charged with delivering test results may have business and technical personnel present. My usual assessment for the ability to communicate at many levels is to ask the candidate about a hobby they have, some topic with a technical basis. Assume I know nothing about the hobby and ground it in something common I may be familiar with. This tests the candidate's ability to think on their feet and speak to audiences of different technical skills.   I am particularly interested in their ability to draw analogies in order to ground concepts and to tie something unknown to the familiar.

Have someone non-technical included as part of the interview process to assess the candidate's ability to communicate effectively with non-technical audiences. While not a premium item for a tool mechanic, a pure performance–test–tool user, this is a critical skill when communicating with outside groups as a person matures into performance engineer and performance architect roles.

Always A Good Story (Or Two Or Three or . . .)

Every solid Performance Architect or Performance Engineer I have crossed paths with since the late 1990s has a few, "That was weird . . .," performance issues in which their efforts were key to identification of the issues. I usually ask for the oddest performance defect they have ever found, the symptoms, and then how the issue was resolved.   Complex issues often require the insight of multiple people to find the final root cause. Key to understanding the value of the candidate is understanding their individual contributions in narrowing the focus of efforts, even to the point of identifying the core issue impacting response time of the ability to scale. The candidate should be able to deliver a compelling story of the identification, the mystery of getting to root cause (including some inevitable false paths), and then finally a resolution. This should be a story they are familiar with, so they should be in their comfort zone as they relate a first hand event even with the nervousness of an interview.

The odd stories stick around precisely because of the difficult nature of finding a resolution to the issue. The easy ones, in contrast, blend into the background of the other easy to solve performance items.

Always check to see if the same story has been published on the Internet. Given the high amount of résumé fraud, introducing cross checks into the process is unfortunately required.

Programming Skills

Ⓐ Ⓔ Ⓣ Ⓢ

Every tool in the market for performance testing use has a scripting language. These range from JavaScript to **C** to **Groovy** to **Pascal** to Java. If the candidate has used multiple tools, then they should be able to effectively compare and contrast which tools leverage which language, which tool/language they prefer, and why. There are very few programming language polymaths in the open market.

Most programmers have a default programming language they prefer to use. My default is 'C.' If forced to switch to a different language, there is an efficiency hit as the developer "composes" in their native language, then transposes to the new one. Sometimes people will select a less optimal tool because they are more optimal in the language used by the tool. The candidate should be able to discuss trade-offs here in labor vs tool efficiency.

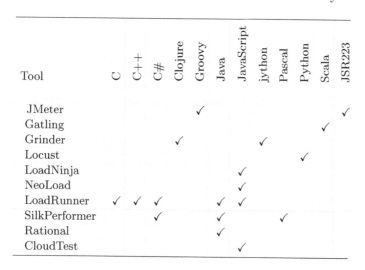

Tool	C	C++	C#	Clojure	Groovy	Java	JavaScript	jython	Pascal	Python	Scala	JSR223
JMeter					✓							✓
Gatling											✓	
Grinder				✓				✓				
Locust										✓		
LoadNinja						✓						
NeoLoad						✓						
LoadRunner	✓	✓	✓		✓	✓						
SilkPerformer		✓			✓				✓			
Rational					✓							
CloudTest					✓							

Figure 4.2: *Common Performance Test Tools & Language Support Table*

You should include someone familiar with the language of the tool in question on your interview team. *Figure 4.2* includes a chart of tools with the languages supported. This will allow you to interview for the tool language skill, even if you are unfamiliar with the tool. For some tools, multiple languages are supported. This may vary by the protocol/interface supported. Because a candidate may not be familiar with every language of a particular tool when multiple languages are supported, you should narrow your inquiry to the applications which are to be tested within your enterprise.

Visual Studio is not noted in the charted set of tools as Microsoft has announced the end-of-life of the performance testing features of Visual Studio. Integrations with Visual Studio are supported by several tools, namely LoadRunner and **SilkPerformer**. These are template solutions, where it is assumed source code for the application will be used. It is expected that tools which support a full integration with Visual Studio will replace the functionality that Microsoft has chosen to terminate.

Project Management Skills

Ⓐ Ⓔ

The building of performance tests is a micro-scale development effort sheltered inside of a larger project. It has all of the same tasks and hallmarks of any other development effort. If requirements have not been collected at the beginning of a project, a requirements collection phase needs to take place. Then a performance test plan may be developed, tests can be constructed (code), quality checked, and finally the test may be executed. Your performance personnel are going to be leading these performance projects, hence the critical nature of project management skills.

An item to take note of for any organization is whether the performance requirements have been available to all areas of the organization since project inception. Have architecture, development, platform engineering, and functional testing efforts been able to leverage the same requirements set as multi-user performance testing efforts? If not, where performance requirements are being collected just prior to performance testing efforts, then consider both project management and communications skills to be critical skills for the organization. *The performance testing effort is going to be using requirements that were never used by any other part of the organization.*

Where performance defects are identified, there will be resistance to the acceptance of the defect. This is genuine and understandable, given that the assumptions used by development and platform engineering will be different than those used by the performance testing team. Developers are naturally defensive of their work, like a parent protecting a child. You might even hear conversation similar to, "Don't call my code (baby) ugly! You need glasses!" Or, "Your tool is broken, your tests are incorrect" (in response to the developer's assumptions).

Scrum masters, product owners, project managers, and development management all need to be involved early if this pattern is present.

Communications skills, mentioned previously, also play a critical role on the defect communications front. A developer requires role and environment appropriate information for the identification and reproduction of issues. Communicate as a project manager to one part of the organization, as a business analyst to a second, as a developer to a third! Not an easy mix to accommodate.

Planning and Budgeting

"Can you have the test scripts done by noon?"

There's likely not an Automated Functional or Performance Tester in an organization which has not heard this question at least once in their career. But it's not necessarily a question asked of traditional developers. For them, the code is done when the code is done.

Performance Engineers and Performance Architects should be able to provide a predictive model for the amount of labor required to fully develop a test set for performance testing purposes.

An example:

> For each Test Script or Protocol X on Tool Y, each test step shall require a budget of Z hours,
> This budgeted test development time shall include:
> - The full development of the script
> - Parameterization of user inputs to vary data
> - Appropriate handling of dynamic data
> - The integration of timing records for the collection of end user response time
> - The handling of error conditions which may be generated by the application under test
> - Checks for expected results in accordance with good test practices

For business functions that are:

- Functionally complete for a single user

- Where a business function scales for a single user

- Where a stable environment exists with isolated data for performance testing

- Seeded with appropriate test data

How's that for a ton of caveats? How does this translate? For a highly skilled user with a tool – given a working business process running on HTTP Web Protocol, without a Rich JavaScript Framework front end — This works out to (roughly) one hour per test step. So, an eight step script clocks in at eight hours. Shorter for some. Longer for others.

If your organization simply sets aside a block of time for performance tests without having a set of requirements and without knowing the labor quotient for a delivery, it will become critical to have a very senior resource to coordinate with other project professionals. Imagine an unstable set of 72 business process scripts being dropped on a performance test team, without a dedicated environment or test data. The expectations are for development within one week, with testing the following week, with a one person test team. It does happen. Something has to give. Usually what "gives" is the quality of the test, with a junior resource leading the effort. Tests often wind up without some business processes represented. Types of tests may be reduced. Risk in production is increased due to reduced insight into the application performance.

Once a performance professional rises to the level of engineer, they should be familiar with this problem of balancing time and labor in the development of test code, as well as the trade offs. This is an excellent reinforcement of their checks for communications skills. It's good to know how well your candidates are able to communicate business risk associated with the compromises that may be made.

Having a project management professional for your organization involved in interviewing should help to uncover weaknesses in this area. Does the candidate need to be a Project Management Professional (**PMP**)? No. But they do need to understand how to budget time and labor for the micro-scale development effort which is the construction and execution of a performance test using a standard set of rules.

Statistics

Performance tests generate substantial volumes of data. This has positive and negative aspects. On a positive basis, wherever we have evidence of acceptable or poor performance, there are typically a large number of confirming samples. The drawbacks? Archiving data does take a substantial amount of disk space. You need tools designed to work with large datasets. You need candidates who understand statistics.

There are several classes of questions which are commonly found across forums for the support of performance testing tools over the past two decades. The first class of questions are generally related to the language of the tool, "How do I program X?" The second class is typically related to tool mechanics, "How do I capture this value coming from the server in tool _____?" The last class being, "What do these numbers mean?" "These numbers" are statistical measurements in reporting results, such as population standard deviation and percentiles.

That these questions continue to show up in public forums is disturbing on many fronts.

a. *Statistics* is a core class taught in the business, math, and computer science programs in universities around the world. This class material has not been retained by individuals, nor have they retained enough knowledge to research the topic directly on the Internet.

b. Statistical information is used in both the construction of load models, representing the behavior of use populations, as well as in the analysis of the test result data. It is easy to have a "garbage in, garbage out" pattern develop with individuals weak with statistics.

The distribution of the response time data can tell us how much a particular request is influenced by a resource dependency. The level of correlation between a change in *response time* and a change in resource usage provides insight into the types of dependencies which are driving the longer response time. Then, when it comes to examine the configuration or application source code, the natural path is to follow to sections of code or system configuration which are biased to the resource in question.

Percentiles are a great normalizing statistic across differing populations. As an example, we can speak of the 90th percentile for the sizes of peaches grown in the state of South Carolina,

my home state. We can also speak about the 90th percentile
for login related to an application. In both cases, it is easy to
understand that ten percent of the values are larger than the
number in question.

We can use percentiles to obtain a feel for the performance of
the majority of the users of the application, limiting the influence
of outliers which may lack high numbers of confirmation samples.
Percentiles are common stats for comparison across tests, both
for examination of test reproducibility as well as for comparison
on before/after changes to the system in question. Performance
requirements traditionally include percentile references related to
response time measurements under load.

If you work in a manufacturing company, pull in someone
from manufacturing quality control to help with the questions
on basic statistics. You may also be able to leverage Six Sigma
Green or Black Belt certified individuals for questions. They
should be versed in statistics as well from their certification
work. Candidates should be able to speak about basic statistical
measures, the use of statistics to uncover trends and patterns
in data, and to demonstrate with white board support for
diagrams. This discussion can act as a confirming sample for
communications skills. Pun intended.

Research Skills

Ⓐ Ⓔ Ⓣ Ⓢ

If there is one constant in the information technology universe
it is change. The pace of change is only accelerating. What does
that mean for anyone in the testing community? It is a virtual
guarantee that in your career you will encounter technologies and
errors which are unique to you and your organization.

For manual testers, the mechanism for interacting with the
application doesn't change all that. For automated testers and
Robotic Process Automation (RPA) software, their set of actions
now includes new models for identification, operation, validation,
and error handling through the interface. For performance testing
— particularly test construction at the protocol level — welcome
to the party! The party will certainly include new and interesting
sets of data flows between client and server. It may even include
new protocols not covered by existing performance testing tools.

HTML as a language is unstructured. What does that mean? Outside of a few structural elements which define the beginning and end of a page, plus some comments, anything goes for how pages are constructed. They can be thin interface veneers, thick JavaScript defined clients, style sheet transformations of structured data, or contain all within the same app in different sections of the interface.

```
<!DOCTYPE html>
<html>
<body>

<!-- This is where unstructured developer
craziness happens -->

</body>
</html>
```

Caution: Geek Stuff

Figure 4.3: *Empty Webpage Example*

JSON & XML payloads bring some structure to the conversation, but it is not guaranteed an application will leverages either standard.

As I have done before, let me ask the obvious question, "Why bring all of this up?" A natural curiosity as to "why" something is constructed in a certain way, along with a desire to find out "how" to effectively test the interface or application is an attribute to seek out. You want those who are not afraid of help files, seeking out data on parallel architecture applications in search engines to understand the source of an error or issue.

There is an observable behavior that is tied to this attribute. Or, perhaps I should label this behavior as an antipattern. Test tool users get stuck in tool usage. Test tool users get stuck in tool execution. Test tool users get stuck when confronted with a "That's weird," and then someone asks, "Why?"

Go to any public forum related to performance testing on any given day and you will find within the most recent posts individuals who are pressed into the role. When stuck, their first inclination is not to research the issue online, not to hit the F1 key for the help file or online documentation. Instead, the first inclination is to simply ask for help in a public forum. All too often these questions are directly addressable by:

a The online tool product documentation.

b An identical question asked multiple times over the past two-and-a-half decades.

c Standards documentation, Requests for Comment (RFC) associated with Internet standards.

There is even a term for a question posted by the same individual to multiple forums simultaneously out of desperation: a shotgun post. Curiosity and research skills fail these individuals.

When you combine this lack of curiosity and poor research skills with an individual who has weak, technical foundational skills, you will wind up with individuals who take five to ten times as long to develop tests and troubleshoot issues. You are looking for a candidate that can research an issue, find an answer, and apply a fix within a short window of time. This is an excellent measure of productivity. Efffective candidates are competing with individuals who should be able to self–solve, but let threads run for days on Facebook, Google Groups, LinkedIn, Stackoverflow, and Yahoo Groups without ever reaching satisfactory resolution. Even at a 100% price premium, a skilled individual who can self–solve becomes a bargain versus someone who takes five to ten times longer, all billed hours, to reach an often poorer-quality state.

During audits of test assets I have found large sections of test code commented out because of individuals unable to solve issues related to tool usage. Why does this matter? Commented out test code points to tests which have not been constructed properly. They have applied incorrect load to the system. The measurement of business risk is incorrect.

These findings are on tests which had been accepted by management as a source of "performance truth." The tests, "PASSED," but only because they were falsely constructed. Only after releasing code to production and the appearance of performance issues were difficult questions asked. These poorly skilled individuals are counting on reporting to stakeholders who lack the technical skills to evaluate their work product beyond a test report which has few (if any) errors.

Find topics that the candidate is unfamiliar with. Topics which are not widely discussed on the Internet. Ask questions. As an organization you want to understand their problem solving capabilities with research. This skill impacts every aspect of performance testing, from test development with a given tool, through researching technical issues related to the diagnosis of *root cause*. Have the candidate walk the interviewers through their research model. Have them demonstrate their skills in asking questions of various sources (documentation, standards, public forums, ...). Ideally, this should be in–person to avoid assistance off–camera in a remote interview model.

Requirements!

"Just make it fast!"

How fast? How many users? What conversion rate? What business transaction mix? What's their site stickiness? This is about as clear as mud and just as dangerous.

Imagine a four–year–old saying they want a new bicycle. This four–year–old has a very specific one in their head. They know the color. They know the pedals — even the color of the pedal reflectors. They know the streamers hanging from the handlebars by color and amount. They even know the degree of sparkliness of the seat.

What happens when you show up with the wrong bike for a four–year–old? "... fast!" What happens next will not be pretty.

Prepare for the organizational equivalent of the four–year–old pitching a fit, with unclear or imprecise performance requirements. Expect challenges from acceptance of defects to uncaptured business risk in deployment. Your candidate should be able to define precisely what constitutes a *Fully Qualified Performance Requirement* (FQPR). They should be able to evaluate a series of requirement examples you produce, providing consistent attribute–based feedback on whether a requirement is sound or not. Is the requirement sufficiently unambiguous? Is it even testable?

For myself, I draw back to the **SMART**[2] acronym, with just enough added color to understand the environment where the requirement is pinned, such as business transactional volume, users, mix of business processes.

Interviewers should be able to present requirements from all over the spectrum. Include examples obviously poor in construction, some very questionable, others rock solid. This is an

---

[2]press.perfbytes.com/books/jp/interview/smart

opportunity for dialog between the candidate and the interviewer to understand how the candidate evaluates such requirements, the rules they use for assessment, and how they communicate gaps from both a business and technology perspective.

Testing Acumen

Ⓐ Ⓔ Ⓣ Ⓢ

Performance testing, in particular multi-user performance testing, is usually one of the last risk gates before deployment. For such a gateway, you want individuals who are solid testers. They should understand the **Scientific Method** quite well. Also, how a performance test aligns with an experiment in the scientific method:

- A Hypothesis, derived from your business and technical requirements that you seek to evaluate.

- A series of reproducible test steps, with expected results. This is for each and every business process.

- A control factor. There are many ways that this can be incorporated into a performance test. This is to test the quality of the test, not the quality of the application. Candidates should be able to walk you through this process.

- Reproducibility. What constitutes a reproducible performance test.

- Observable results.

- Reporting findings.

Testing is, at it's core, a process. This is true whether it is a performance test of a car, a physics experiment, or a software test. There are common attributes in the experiment which need to be present. Your candidate should be able to identify poorly designed tests, both inside and outside of the software realm.

A screening question which I have commonly used includes a test of an automobile running from 0-100 mph. I will change some variables between test executions, and then ask whether it is valid to compare the two tests, "Why, or why not?" I will then switch to a software test, changing a similar number of variables, then asking the same question. The answers should be similar in response. More often than not the answers are different for interviews I have conducted over the years. This is very telling for a candidate, on both the issues of being able to think abstractly on process items, and predictive for testing acumen.

I realize, by sharing the above, I have spoiled the screening ability of such a question. Interviewers should endeavor, as part of candidate examination, to come up with a series of questions to evaluate the candidate's testing acumen. Do not consider credentials with a testing organization as a substitute for your own examination, with your own in-house experts. It is unfortunately the case that banks of test questions[3] are available for standardized industry credentials in much the same way as banks of interview questions[4] are also available.

A poorly skilled tester increases your risk in deployment, which is precisely the opposite of what organizations seek: To reduce risk in deployment.

Tool Skill vs Human Skill

Ⓐ Ⓔ Ⓣ

In the forward of this book I noted my time with Mercury Interactive, along with their famous sales slogan, "... with this tool..." It is time to tackle this issue of what a tool can do versus what a human can do. A performance testing tool can only provide data for analysis.

Where a person understands how to use the data in order to reveal the behavior of systems being tested, there is a path to value in delivery. The test data will allow for the identification of issues related to slow response times and scalability. Additionally, the data can provide reinforcement for recommendations, or findings, on the performance of the system. Findings derived from test data are the basis for adjustments to configuration, or sections of code. In the long run, the findings justify changes to the architecture of the application to improve performance.

For individuals who are not able to troubleshoot complex systems today, a tool will not provide them with this additional capability. *I expect to receive a lot of difficult emails for that last statement from tool vendors.*

These are individuals who are charged with the use of a performance testing tool, but who lack the skills to identify issues, who have not had the benefit of training or a mentor in this discipline. Having a tool to generate data only enables them to generate data. Lots of data. That's it — End of capability. The generated timing record and monitoring data lacks context, which comes from the training and mentoring efforts.

---

[3]`press.perfbytes.com/books/jp/interview/testquestions`
[4]`press.perfbytes.com/books/jp/interview/interviewquestions`

When this happens analysis of system performance for the identification of performance issues inevitably becomes the responsibility of others within the organization.   An updated description from Mercury, if they were still around, should be, "...with this tool, anyone can generate data, lots & lots of data..." It still takes a skilled individual to analyze the data for issues and resolutions.

I know. This is not anywhere near as short and sexy as the Mercury Interactive product demo. It doesn't remove barriers to the sale. The truth can be quite ugly.

Futures

This challenge in test analysis will not always be forever present in the market. Application performance analysis is a discipline that lends itself well to pattern recognition. Already, companies are leveraging this close match of performance to pattern in order to identify items which cause performance to improve or decline.

Companies such as **Akamas** and Dynatrace are on the cutting edge of pattern recognition and the application of changes to improve performance.   Both companies are employing similar approaches in the identification of resources in use and response times to recommend changes to the systems being monitored. You might recall viewing a **Davis** demonstration from Dynatrace PERFORM conference which highlights this, "Hey, I have found something. Shall I fix it?" approach.

Akamas takes the model one step further.   They leverage machine learning associated with unknown, but similar patterns observed at customer locations.   Then, Akamas' solution set can proactively experiment in the system to arrive at higher performing configurations of software, leveraging the educated guesses from machine learning. Each new positive reinforcement educates the machine learning algorithm with additional data points. This results in system configurations that a human would take years to arrive at with A/B testing. These configurations can be extremely odd looking. What is inarguable is the extremely well–tuned performance (scalability and response times) for the application and workload combination.

To leverage either model in a pre–production sense mandates the ability to both model workloads effectively and to build tests that accurately produce load on the system in question. Akamas' auto tuning cannot work effectively on a pre–production basis if the workload is wrong. Dynatrace similarly will not be able to identify problematic patterns where a workload doesn't trigger a rule in test.

Whether you have sophisticated tools such as Akamas or not, if the test design & execution are incorrect, then you will know shortly after releasing to production. "Issues" will begin to appear, caught and reported by production monitoring systems. Your production help desk is considered a production monitoring system — solid releases have fewer issues. The live user population behavior will begin triggering notifications.

While the need for analysis skills will benefit from strong tool complements going forward, the need for architecture skills to uncover deeper patterns in design, the ability to design tests which model load effectively, and sound tool skills will remain.

(Finally) That Tool Thing

Ⓐ Ⓔ Ⓣ

As noted earlier, open–source tools are like Lego components. You pull a load generator from one tool, a monitoring solution from a second/third tool, reporting from another. plugging these components together results in a solution. Commercial tools are monolithic stacks, having load generation, monitoring collection, and analysis inside of the same tool family.

Candidates should be able to discuss the difference in the capability of tools they have used, particularly in monitoring and analysis capabilities, where value is delivered. Someone who sees no difference in out–of–the–box capability for open–source and commercial tools is a large red flag. They will typically collect response time data, then consider the work complete.

Open-ended, compare–and–contrast type questions should be the norm here. Candidates should be able to make comparisons within a tool, for different protocols, or across tools in terms of capabilities. Also, how they have used such capabilities shows their experience and versatility with different tools. Anything noted on their résumé is fair game.

Examples:

- I see you have tool X and tool Y in your background. Could you compare the monitoring and analysis capabilities of these tools?

- You note both **TruClient** and HTTP protocol use at your last project. Why didn't you just go with one over the other?

- Can you compare the collection of dynamic data from servers using Tool X and Tool Y for the HTTP Protocol?

- (variant) Can you compare the collection of dynamic data from servers using HTTP and Database virtual users for LoadRunner, as you have noted use for both on your résumé?

- Make your strongest technical argument for the use of both Tool X and Tool Y for the testing of this application architecture. (Have a sheet available with a diagram of all of the architectural components, but with some information missing, such as the use of a front end JavaScript framework, the name of the database, ... You are looking for both questions and their best arguments.)

It's difficult to provide a formula for what these open-ended types of questions look like, as they are always drawn from the candidate's direct résumé. I will make a deal with you: If you send a résumé to `mailto:openquestions@press.perbytes.com`, I will draw one open–ended question from each résumé and post it as part of a support file for this book. This will be downloadable from **press.perfbytes.com**.

I always pick two to three items to follow up from the responses to open-ended questions. This activity is to probe for depth with the candidate, such as "You mentioned , 'X.' Could you go into some detail on how that piece is configured or used as part of your testing?" For people who interview often, the areas to probe are often obvious. Be wary when candidates are seeking confirmation on their answers with the interviewer.

If a candidate has rock-solid foundational skills with proper mentoring they can be effective in a short duration. This is true even if they have never touched a performance testing tool in their life. Under or around 30 days would be typical for such a candidate. If a candidate is weak in all foundational skills, plus some weak tool skills, they will struggle to deliver value in performance testing services for years. It is not uncommon to find people operating in performance testing roles for five years or more without delivering anything more than response time data from a tool generated report to other parts of the enterprise.

Open–Source vs Commercial capabilities

Referring back to the tools noted earlier, Figure 4.2 on page 30 contains a list of capabilities for each tool. I have also included **BlazeMeter**, **Flood.IO** and **OctoPerf** in this list of capabilities. These solutions exist to fill in the gaps associated with open–source tools which make them difficult to scale. To date, the analysis solutions from these vendors have not reached similar levels of maturity as their historic commercial offerings.

Figure 4.4 keys

✓ Full capability.

[I] Immature capability compared to historic commercial tools.

[R] Client–based, response time, errors, load generator health items

[3] Third–party integration required for capability.

[B] Benchmark Standard.

Tool	Scripting	Test Design	Monitoring	Analysis	Reporting	DevOps Pipeline
JMeter	✓	✓	[3]	[3]	[R]	✓
Gatling	✓	✓	[3]	[3]	[R]	✓
Grinder	✓	✓	[3]	[3]	[R]	✓
Locust	✓	✓	[3]	[3]	[R]	✓
LoadNinja	✓	✓	[3]	[I]	[R]	✓
NeoLoad	✓	✓	✓	✓	✓	✓
LoadRunner	✓	✓	[B]	[B]	[B]	✓
SilkPerformer	✓	✓	✓	✓	✓	✓
Rational	✓	✓	✓	✓	✓	✓
CloudTest	✓	✓	✓	✓	✓	[B]
BlazeMeter	✓	✓	✓	[I]	✓	✓
Flood.IO	✓	✓	✓	[I]	✓	✓
OctoPerf	[B]	✓	✓	[I]	✓	✓

Figure 4.4: *Common Tools & Feature Support*

The [B] benchmark standard players include a substantial number of first–mover advantages. You can see classical LoadRunner here for the integrated monitoring developed over almost three decades; plus it's analysis and reporting, which still set the benchmark for other tools. An [I] immature in Monitoring and Analysis is in direct reference to capabilities similar to those of LoadRunner. Akamai **CloudTest** has a substantial first–mover advantage on the DevOps pipeline front. From the outset,

CloudTest was the first tool on the commercial market to embrace DevOps, with a seamless integration into the existing market frameworks.   OctoPerf has built a superb script development interface into their product versus the other, "We'll take your open–source tool script and run with it," vendors. And, for that capability they deserve recognition.

Open–source tools also place a premium on programming skills. These are tools designed by developers, built by developers, with the intended use by developers. Bringing in a person with weak programming skills will not serve the organization well when paired with an open–source tool.

Closing Out The Foundations

It will be rare that you find someone strongly skilled in all areas, as these would tend to be to very senior engineers or architects.   It is far more likely you will find a mix of strengths and weaknesses in individual candidates. Hopefully you can pair individuals who possess complementary areas of strength and weakness for delivery.   The fewer the number of people on the team, the greater the need for a more advanced set of skills (and price in market).

Referred to in the chapter on <u>The Performance Test</u>, with a few process changes almost every organization can pick up about eighty percent of the performance issues you would find with traditional performance testing inside of unit and functional tests. The few changes are:

1. Solid performance requirements at project inception —This allows for the creation of performance budgets related to time and resources allowed for each tier and each unit of code.

2. Ask a performance question, either on time or resources, every time a functional set of questions is asked at the Unit, Component Assembly or Functional states.

3. Seek to passively collect response times throughout the system using logs and Real User Monitor (**RUM**) JavaScript add–ins for web-based applications. This log and RUM data can be collected in a variety of tools, such as AppDynamics, **Datadog**, Dynatrace, **ElasticStack**, **New Relic**, **Splunk**, to name a few. Profiling the response time requests will result in identification of performance issues early in development when the accumulated technical debt is low. This results in an easier fix to the software in question.

Nearly all organizations silo performance questions to a small group near the end of the development process where they can have the least impact on code going out the door. By asking questions earlier and more consistently, you have the luxury of earlier discovery, closer to the point of introduction and cheaper to fix.

As noted previously, the fewer the number of individuals on your testing team the higher the number of core, foundational skills you need to have vested in each individual. Will every individual have every skill to the same level of maturity? That is unlikely. But knowing the relative weaknesses and strengths of candidates will allow you to build teams of individuals with complementary weaknesses and strengths.

As teams grow beyond half a dozen individuals specialization can begin to take place. This is especially beneficial on the bottom end of the skills spectrum for performance testers, grounded in tool mechanics. This allows an organization the luxury of hiring specialized tool users, with planning and analysis taking place amongst more mature engineering resources. This also provides for a natural pipeline of in-house mentoring and maturing of Performance Testers to become Performance Engineers, Performance Engineers grow into Performance Architects. As rare as these performance skills are in the marketplace, having an in–house model for growing more sophisticated capabilities provides an organization with a competitive market advantage on skills.

The Chart!

Here is a quick chart for each of the core skills and which role should have developed expertise. Consider this a cheat sheet of the areas to cover as part of your interview process. Combine these foundational skills in 4.5, with the Role Capabilities Table (*Figure 2.2*) for a comprehensive view of topics and skills to assess against candidates.

Foundation Skill	Tester	Engineer	Architect	SRE
Architecture		✓	✓	✓
Communications		✓	✓	
Programming Skills	✓	✓	✓	✓
Project Mgmt		✓	✓	
Statistics		✓	✓	
Research Skills	✓	✓	✓	✓
Requirements		✓	✓	
Testing Acumen	✓	✓	✓	✓
Tools	✓	✓	✓	

Figure 4.5: *Role Foundation Skills Table*

5

Challenges

This chapter is about the market items that are impacting the ability to deliver value in performance services today. Some of them may be obvious, some tragic, & some hilarious in execution. Each one contributes to the process of finding a skilled individual that much more difficult.

Online Banks of Questions

As a moderator for various forums related to performance testing, performance engineering, and software quality assurance, I found myself removing posts on a weekly basis which contain banks of interview questions[1] collected that are related to performance testing interviews. For good measure, I also ban the users from the site and ban their access to other sites when the identity is common across sites. This is a never-ending task, curbing people trying to game the hiring process.

These banks of questions have resulted in an odd relationship developing between interviewer and candidate for many companies. This is particularly true when the availability of a skilled performance professional is non-existent among interview candidates. Insufficiently skilled candidates wind up studying

---

[1] press.perfbytes.com/books/jp/interview/interviewquestions

45

the same bank of interview questions as the interviewers, who are trying to obtain background in an exotic subject before an interview takes place.

Consider the following: A question is asked of a candidate. It is answered with a close, if not exact, match to the answer the interviewer found online. The candidate winds up being hired. Six months later, the candidate is let go. Rather than hire a firm to interview, the process often repeats. This leads to multiple generations of poor performance personnel, one following the other. As rates follow value, it becomes increasingly difficult for the hiring manager to justify market rates for skilled candidates, where the interviewed & hired candidates continue to deliver low value.

You would be well advised to concentrate on core foundational skills, combined with some tool questions of your own design. Base questions upon the candidate's résumé, rather than use online banks of questions for hiring purposes. The odds are high that an immature candidate will have found the same questions to study. Incorrect answers have been seeded into online question banks as control questions by skilled professionals. This helps interviewers determine if a candidate is genuine or not, resulting in perfect incorrect responses to studied questions.

My advice? Do not use a published interview question for a hiring decision.

"Meat Puppet"

Contract IT labor has always had a bit of Wild West flavor to it. Over the years, I have seen items as varied as bait & switch from phone interview to who shows up in person, outright resume fraud, paid phone referral banks, and background impersonation by firms placing someone else's name at the top of a résumé. Heck, I have even received my own résumé back with someone else's name at the top. I am not the only person to which this has happened. I did interview the candidate, for entertainment purposes only. I do not think the candidate or the representing firm were entertained.

In early 2018, something new appeared. Because of bait & switch fraud with phone candidates, firms switched to video interviews of candidates. The COVID work–from–home dictates have further reinforced video interviews. This makes perfect sense when you consider that now you have a face and voice to match to the person who shows up to do the work, either remotely in a Zoom meeting or on-site. This new item involves an alteration of the video-stream to the candidate.

Firms representing candidates have been using software to alter the bitrate for cameras during interviews. Injecting network errors into the stream creates what appears to be genuine network issues. At the same time, the interview candidate sits in a chair in front of the screen *appearing* to answer questions. Off-screen, another individual is addressing the questions asked, while the candidate in front of the screen is attempting to move their mouth in unison with the speaker. Because of the "network issues" you wind up with an occasional lip-sync parody of a Kung Fu film dubbed into English.[2]

"Meat Puppet!"

If you are in a video interview with a poor network connection and find the lips of the candidate on screen don't quite line up with what is being said, be suspicious. Be very suspicious. Reschedule. Bring it to the attention of your recruiter and HR. Investigate the supplier for evidence of bait & switch on skills from this firm before rescheduling, such as, "great technical interview, but the candidate seems to be struggling once integrated with the project." This is a coordinated activity. If found, your organization should blackball the provider firm from further consideration.

In–Person Interviews

When hiring an individual who will be charged with building and executing performance tests, include an in-person practical examination of their skills when possible. Similar to the "Meat Puppet" problem, remote exams are not always an accurate predictor of capabilities.

I recommend scheduling a half–day. Be sure that the task cannot be completed in total for the period of time allotted, but substantial progress can be made. Do not include all of the information or data needed to complete the task. This is a test of technical skills, communications skills, and a willingness to enquire about missing data/information requisite for success.

Examples:

- Script creation against your application for a known difficult business process.

---

[2] `https://www.youtube.com/watch?v=1pFjpfmeOtg`

- Analysis of test results. Candidate is given an hour and half to go through test results to make recommendations based upon the data presented. Candidate will need to present their analysis to other team members. It is optimal if the results contain an issue where a monitor picks up symptoms of the root cause.

- Analysis of existing performance requirements for gaps in understanding/clarity. You might consider modifying requirements if your organization has clear and concise performance requirements. All levels of performance personnel should be able to identify poor requirements for testing.

Social Promotion

2011 WASHINGTON DC -"Go home. I want you to watch LoadRunner videos on YouTube. When you come back in the morning be prepared to be a part of the performance test efforts."

I witnessed this very conversation between an on-site engagement manager and an excellent functional automation specialist. This example of social promotion is a continuation of the power of statements by Mercury Interactive's sales team as early as 1996, "...with our tool..." The outcome of that direction was as you might expect. Not good. The firm in question did get to bill a government client a very large amount for a *skilled* performance tester. Billing was more important than value in delivery for this engagement manager.

Management at many tiers in companies would like to believe that substantial portions of information technology are commoditized; that the difference in value between the least and greatest cost just isn't that great. Cheapest wins! This does, in the end, become a self-fulfilling prophesy as low value in delivery leads to low rates to match value. Skill levels for people are only substantially similar at the least skilled and the most skilled ends of the spectrum. People's skills are highly differentiated at the layers in between.

If your firm is one which prefers to promote from within, there is a model with a proven track record of producing a skilled Performance Engineer:

1. Shore up the candidate's foundational skills, including training or mentoring if needed.

2. Send the candidate to tool training, with a credentialed instructor if available.

3. Provide a mentor for a period of time until the person can lead engagements on their own. The amount of time required is directly proportional to the strength of the foundational skills. Someone showing up with two decades of refined foundational skills can be effective within 30 days, as the skill gap amounts to tool knowledge and a few process items. People with substantial gaps in foundational skills may require mentoring for upwards of a year before they are effective.

You may elect to deviate from this strategy if you have someone with all of the solid, foundational skills. These individuals already have a strong track record diagnosing performance issues. For these already skilled individuals, you have just provided a greater capacity to generate data for analysis.

For all other individuals the track record of deviating from the above model is clear. A person who struggles with using tools for years will have an associated low–value delivery. You will find these individuals on sites all over the Internet. They will be asking questions about basic tool usage covered in training, spending days to solve problems which should take an hour or less. The picture is not pretty.

Exit Strategy

Quality Assurance has acquired a reputation over the past two plus decades as a starter field for a career. Career advancement is seen as moving to development, project management, or personnel management to show career progression. As with many starter roles, this tends to occur at the three-to-five year mark. This is just about the point where performance engineers become very effective.

Performance Engineering has a strong basis in patterns of resource use, patterns of behavior, and architectural patterns. While a mentor can help introduce patterns to individuals, Information Technology professionals tend to learn best through hands–on experience, versus reading or listening to information on a topic. The performance professional's exposure to multiple systems over a period of time helps to build this "pattern library," and cultivate an architectural view of systems. This pattern development and understanding is key to the identification of performance issues. Individuals who stay in the performance field beyond five years, particularly ones with a strong track record of issue identification, are market gems.

Antipatterns & Candidates

It is the desire of most organizations to pay the least amount of money to get the maximum possible benefit. In the case of software performance professionals the words of John Ruskin, 19th century poet, should ring loud and clear,

> *"...When you pay too little, you sometimes lose everything, because the thing you bought was incapable of doing the thing it was bought to do. The common law of business balance prohibits paying a little and getting a lot — it can't be done. ..."* - John Ruskin[3]

Be wary of what is cheap. For many years, I would receive phone calls from offshore vendors offering me highly-skilled LoadRunner engineers at less than $20 per hour. Interviews revealed that the resources were worth less than a dollar per hour in actual skills. And yet, these organizations were enormously successful at selling their services with a long reference list. This again emphasizes the problem of managers being unable to recognize the skills required for the job, unable to recognize value in the delivery, and accepting the premise of commoditization driven by vendors, "... with this tool..."

---

[3]https://www.lifeofanarchitect.com/john-ruskin-common-law-of-business-balance/

Last Word

Thank you for taking the time to read this book. I hope you have found something of value here which will help you find a candidate well suited for your software performance needs. Since the late 1990s these techniques have been used to identify individuals who are already in the field to hire for engagements, as well for the identification of individuals with the right foundation skills to bring into the industry with a high chance of success

I fully expect that this book will be purchased by individuals on both sides of the interview process. It is my hope that this results in a far more difficult process for those who are engaging in skills–fraud in attempting to obtain employment.

If you need assistance in the interview process for a performance candidate please reach out to PerfBytes for assistance — `mailto:interviewhelp@perfbytes.com`. We will place you in touch with an architect–level individual who can help interview and vet your candidates. This is with the full and transparent understanding that the interview effort is the service to be delivered.

Until we meet again, happy hiring!

Appendix

Figure 4.3 Support Data

Apache JMeter

R Reporting
press.perfbytes.com/books/jp/interview/jmeterreporting
3 Analysis
Documentation is silent
3 Monitoring
Documentation is silent

Gatling

R Reporting
press.perfbytes.com/books/jp/interview/gatlingreports
3 Analysis
Documentation is silent
3 Monitoring
press.perfbytes.com/books/jp/interview/gatlingmonitoring

Locust

R Reporting
press.perfbytes.com/books/jp/interview/locustreports
3 Analysis
Documentation is silent
3 Monitoring
Documentation is silent

SmartBear LoadNinja

R Reporting
press.perfbytes.com/books/jp/interview/SBreports
I Analysis
press.perfbytes.com/books/jp/interview/SBanalysis

[3]   **Monitoring**
Documentation is silent

Micro Focus LoadRunner

[B]   **Reporting**
`press.perfbytes.com/books/jp/interview/LRreports`
[B]   **Analysis**
`press.perfbytes.com/books/jp/interview/LRanalysis`
[B]   **Monitoring**
`press.perfbytes.com/books/jp/interview/LRmonitor`

Akamai CloudTest

[B]   **CI/CD DevOps**
`press.perfbytes.com/books/jp/interview/CTdevops`

CA BlazeMeter

[I]   **Analysis/Reporting**
`press.perfbytes.com/books/jp/interview/BMreports`

Tricentis Flood.io

[I]   **Analysis/Reporting**
`press.perfbytes.com/books/jp/interview/Floodreports`

Octoperf

[I]   **Analysis**
`press.perfbytes.com/books/jp/interview/OPreports`
[B]   **Scripting**
`press.perfbytes.com/books/jp/interview/OPscripting`

Glossary

Agile Development model. commonly aligned to DevOps. see **press.** `perfbytes.com/books/jp/interview/agile.`

Akamas Software Development Company. Performance Engineering. See `press.perfbytes.com/books/jp/interview/akamas.`

autoscaling The ability of a cloud based virtual machine to expand the available resources for CPU and Memory available to a virtualized host under high load conditions where such resources are being consumed at a high rate..

Banyan Located in Westboro, MA. Builder of the Vines network operating system, underpinned by StreetTalk, the first globally accessible directory service used by both users and administrators of the network for the identification and management of network objects. Defunct.

BlazeMeter Hosting company for execution of performance tests. See `press.perfbytes.com/books/jp/interview/blazemeter.`

Business Process A defined set of steps whose output supports a business function, such as completing the sale of an item, requesting a new password, or on-boarding an employee. For performance testing, this is a documented set of steps to be completed to model the behavior of a user, or users, who are interacting with a piece of software..

C Programming Language, see `press.perbytes.com/books/jp/interview/Clang.`

C++ Programming Language, see `press.perfbytes.com/books/jp/interview/Cpluslang.`

C# Programming Language, see `press.perfbytes.com/books/jp/interview/Csharp.`

Clojure Programming Language, see `press.perfbytes.com/books/jp/interview/clojure.`

CloudTest Commercial Software produced by Akamai. Formerly of SOASTA software Performance Testing. See `press.perfbytes.com/books/jp/interview/cloudtest.`

Datadog Commercial Software. Monitoring software. See **press.** `perfbytes.com/books/jp/interview/datadog.`

Davis The Voice Interface for Dynatrace. See `press.perfbytes.com/books/jp/interview/davis.`

deep diagnostic A class of tools characterized by the ability to peer inside of the source code execution of a Java or .Net virtual machine. This allows for the execution costs of a section of code to be examined directly by statistics collected by the deep diagnostic tool. Examples: AppDynamics, Dynatrace, New Relic, Wily Introscope, Micro Focus Diagnostics.

Dynatrace Software Company. Producer of application and system performance management and monitoring too. See `press.perfbytes.com/books/jp/interview/dynatrace`.

ElasticStack Open–Source Software. Elastisearch, Logstash, Kibana. Used for the processing and display of information from machine data (logs). See `press.perfbytes.com/books/jp/interview/elastic`.

finite resource pool The limit of CPU,Disk, Memory, & Network associated with a given host. This limit may be physical or virtual in nature. Virtual limits may be changed on the fly, up to, but not exceeding the limits of the physical resources on a host. Also termed the Four Horsemen of Application Performance by Scott Moore[4].

Flood Hosting company for execution of performance tests. See `press.perfbytes.com/books/jp/interview/flood`.

foundation skills The skills you have before you begin to make use of performance testing tools effectively. See chapter, **Foundation Skills**.

Furman A small, liberal arts college located outside of Greenville, SC. Find out more at `www.furman.edu`.

Ganymede Software Manufacturer of Layer 7 network performance testing tool, Chariot and network monitoring tool Pegasus. Testing tools now a part of Ixia..

Gatling Open–Source Software. Performance Testing Tool , see `press.perfbytes.com/books/jp/interview/gatling`.

Gigalabs Located in Silicon Valley. Manufacturer of HPPI, HSSI super computing interfaces and routers. Defunct.

Google Groups Email lists maintains be google to include historic USENET email lists as well as newer topic driven lists. See *Yahoo Groups*..

Grafana Open–Source dashboard visualization software, see `press.perfbytes.com/books/jp/interview/grafana`.

Grinder Open–Source Software. Performance Testing Framework , see `press.perfbytes.com/books/jp/interview/grinder`.

Groovy Programming Language, see `press.perfbytes.com/books/jp/interview/groovy`.

Java Developed initially by Sun. Now owned and Maintained by ORACLE Corporation. A cross platform development language characterized by a software virtual machine which abstracts the underlying OS and Hardware from the programmer. This allows for a high degree of code portability between systems leveraging the same Java code base. For more information on Java, see `press.perfbytes.com/books/jp/interview/java`).

JavaScript A scripting language support by modern browsers which may be used to build intelligent client applications delivered via HTTP web protocol. Also used by Node.JS as a server side scripting language for the construction of responses to requests. See, `press.perfbytes.com/books/jp/interview/javascript`.

JMeter An open–source performance testing tool from the Apache Foundation. Available at `press.perfbytes.com/books/jp/interview/jmeter`.

jython Programming Language, see `press.perfbytes.com/books/jp/interview/jython`.

---

[4]`press.perfbytes.com/books/jp/interview/scottmoore`

Load Profile A model of end user behaviors used as a basis for a load test. The model will consist of the business functions to be executed, the number of times the business process should be completed within an hour, the number of users engaged in the process.

LoadNinja Commercial Software produced by SmartBear Software. See `press.perfbytes.com/books/jp/interview/loadninja`.

LoadRunner Commercial Software produced by Micro Focus Software. Performance Testing. See `press.perfbytes.com/books/jp/interview/loadrunner`.

Locust Open–Source Software. Performance Testing Tool. See `press.perfbytes.com/books/jp/interview/locust`.

Log Analysis Leveraging logs to profile the behavior of users or systems. Logs are an objective set of data for how users are navigating systems. As such, the are considered an input to a load profile..

machine learning An algorithmic model for finding similar patterns based upon a prior set of patterns used to "train" an algorithm. The larger the training set, the easier it becomes to spot similar patterns. See `press.perfbytes.com/books/jp/interview/ml`.

Maslow (Abraham) Psychologist. Examined the base driver's for human behavior, See `press.perfbytes.com/books/jp/interview/maslow`.

Mercury Manufacturer of application testing tools for quality assurance organization. Notorious for an options backdating scandal involving executives. Assets sold to Hewlett Packard. Testing tools now a part of Micro Focus..

Micro Focus Software Company. Known first for Micro Focus COBOL, has acquired the testing assets of CompuWare. Mercury Interactive, Segue Software. Currently produces LoadRunner and SilkPerformer See `press.perfbytes.com/books/jp/interview/microfocus`.

Microsoft Make of operating systems and applications, from desktop to cloud. For more information, `www.microsoft.com`.

Moore's Law Opined by Intel Research Scientist Gordon Moore, holds that computing power doubles every 18 months at the same price point. See, `press.perfbytes.com/books/jp/interview/mooreslaw`.

NeoLoad Commercial Performance Testing tool. Developed by Tricentis Software. See `press.perfbytes.com/books/jp/interview/neoload`.

New Relic Commercial Software. Manufacturer of web hosted deep diagnostic software. See `press.perfbytes.com/books/jp/interview/newrelic`.

NIST National Institute of Standards & Technology. Part of the United States Department of Commerce. Engages in basic research and defines standards across a wide array of technologies. See `www.nist.gov/`.

OctoPerf Hosting company for execution of performance tests. See `press.perfbytes.com/books/jp/interview/octoperf`.

open–source A development and distribution model for software where the source code for the application/device is made available for modification by the end user of the software/item. This is commonly paired with the GNU licensing model as part of the FOSS, or Free and Open–Source Software, initiative.

PaaS Platform as a Service. Typically managed in-house..

Pascal Programming Language, see `press.perfbytes.com/books/jp/interview/pascal`.

PerfBytes Founded by James Pulley & Mark Tomlinson as a series of podcasts to help improve the value of services delivered related to software performance engineering. 2021 expansion to include video and a publishing operation. PerfBytes Press is the publisher of this book. Find out more at `www.perfbytes.com`.

Performance Architect Super-set of Performance Engineer skills. Is a performance professional who is able to identify areas of risk at the design and business requirements stages, with the ability to make recommendations which reduce risk and improve performance of the application..

Performance Engineer Super-set of Performance Tester skills. Is a performance professional who works with the business to define requirements, designs tests to meet those requirements and analyzes the results of tests for issues. Often a performance engineer can make recommendations to improve performance without ever running a test based upon observations collected from functional tests or production. Performance engineers are data driven..

Performance Test A broad category of tests which are concerned with response time of a system, or scalability of the system related to the use of finite resources. Performance tests may be conducted as early as single execution of a unit test where performance budgets have been constructed to allow the individual developer to understand how much time and/or resources the individual unit function is allowed at maximum..

Performance Tester Is a performance professional who is capable of producing a test from a set of requirements. This individual doesn't necessarily have the skills to collect and vet requirements, nor analyze test data for root cause. They are well versed in tool mechanical skills.

PMP Project Management Professional Certification. See `press.perfbytes.com/books/jp/interview/pmp`.

Prometheus Open–Source monitoring Framework Software, see `press.perfbytes.com/books/jp/interview/prometheus`.

Python Programming Language, see `press.perfbytes.com/books/jp/interview/python`.

R R is both a language and a statistical package for the statistical processing of data, along with visualization of the output, see `press.perfbytes.com/books/jp/interview/rproject`.

RAIL Response Animation Idle Load, see `press.perfbytes.com/books/jp/interview/rail`.

Rational Rational Performance Tester. Commercial Software produced by IBM. Performance Testing. See `press.perfbytes.com/books/jp/interview/rpt`.

React A JavaScript library/framework for building rich user interfaces which execute inside of the client browser. See, `press.perfbytes.com/books/jp/interview/react`.

resource leak An allocation of a resource for which no corresponding deallocation exists. For C, this is when a memory allocation takes place using a variant of *alloc() without a corresponding free() statement on the memory handle. For Java, this occurs when a variable is initialized and seeded with a value, but the memory location is not set to NULL, allowing for the garbage collector to reallocate the memory for use. Memory allocation also applies to connection handles for network and disk activities. Orphaned connections which are not cleaned up can result in the inability to connect to external hosts or disks to write data..

response time A capture of time, typically in milliseconds, to note the completion of a response associated with a request to a system. The response time may be as small as an individual request and response or as large as a complex web page containing hundreds of elements that need to be satisfied for the page to render and become usable..

root cause The source of a Performance Issue, associated with the use and management of resources by code, or configuration of a system. "Getting to root cause," means to find the source of an issue. With that, a path to a resolution. This is the core value proposition for performance testing. Finding issues, and then isolation to root cause..

RUM Real User Monitor. An embedded JavaScript or Browser add-in which collects statistics associated with the world wide web consortium (w3c) Navtiming standard. See `press.perfbytes.com/books/jp/interview/rumnav`.

SaaS Software as a Service. Typically managed by the software provider. Often limits are placed on the amount of load which can be applied to the system during performance tests to reduce the opportunity for impact to other tenants of the system. Visibility into resources is limited. Rarely are response time commitments incorporated into contracts for SaaS providers..

Scala Programming Language, see `press.perfbytes.com/books/jp/interview/scala`.

Scaled Agile Development and Business Organizational model. See `press.perfbytes.com/books/jp/interview/scaledagile`.

Scientific Method A structured process for scientific inquiry. See `press.perfbytes.com/books/jp/interview/science`.

SilkPerformer Commercial Software produced by Micro Focus Software. Performance Testing. See `press.perfbytes.com/books/jp/interview/silkperformer`.

SLA Acronym, Service Level Agreement. A contractual agreement associated with the up-time or response time of a system. SaaS and PaaS Providers rarely commit to a response time SLA unless pressed as part of contract negotiations. Standard agreements for SaaS and PaaS cover up-time..

SMART Acronym related to the specificity of a requirement. See `press.perfbytes.com/books/jp/interview/smart`.

Splunk Commercial Software. Used for the processing and display of machine data. See `press.perfbytes.com/books/jp/interview/splunk`.

SQAForums *Also known as QAForums.* Before the explosion of special interest forums on LinkedIn and Facebook, SQAForums was the default location for people to turn to for questions on Software Quality Assurance processes and tools. See `www.sqaforums.com`.

SRE Systems Reliability Engineer. An individual who splits time between development and operations in support of a piece of software in a DevOps organizational model. Pioneered by Google. See `press.perfbytes.com/books/jp/interview/sre`.

Tableau Commercial Software. Analytics and data visualization platform, see `press.perfbytes.com/books/jp/interview/tableau`.

TEK TEK Systems is the largest provider of Information Technology Labor in North America. TEK Global Services is the solution arm of TEK System. See `press.perfbytes.com/books/jp/interview/TEK`.

timing record A user defined measurement of time collected on an automated basis by a testing tool.

transaction see, *timing record*.

TruClient LoadRunner Protocol. Full Browser Testing Interface..

Visual Studio Integrated Development Environment for multiple languages supported by Microsoft. See `press.perfbytes.com/books/jp/ interview/vstudio`.

VMware Commercial Hypervisor Software for building private clouds inside of companies. See `press.perfbytes.com/books/jp/interview/vmware`.

Waterfall Development mode, see `press.perfbytes.com/books/jp/ interview/waterfall`.

Yahoo Groups Email lists managed by Yahoo on a variety of topics of interest to users.

Index

No sentient beings were harmed in the creation
of this book.

CPSIA information can be obtained
at www.ICGtesting.com
Printed in the USA
BVHW020913181121
621923BV00017B/595

9 780988 540262